HOW IT HAPPENS
at the Ice Cream Factory

By Shawndra Shofner
Photographs by Bob and Diane Wolfe

CLARA HOUSE BOOKS

Minneapolis

The publisher would like to thank the employees of Kemps LLC for their generous help with this book. Thanks as well to Bob King and his staff for welcoming us to photograph in their store. All photogaphs by Bob and Diane Wolfe with the following exceptions: p. 3, Drew Schwartzhoff, p. 30 and back cover, Kemps.

Clara House Books
The Oliver Press, Inc.
Charlotte Square
5707 West 36th Street
Minneapolis, MN 55416-2510

Publisher Cataloging Information
Shofner, Shawndra
      How it happens at the ice cream factory / by Shawndra Shofner ; photographs by Bob and Diane Wolfe.
          p.   cm.
      Includes index.
      ISBN 978-1-934545-06-5
      Summary: Text and photographs describe the ingredients, machinery, and processes used to make different kinds of ice cream.
      1. Ice cream, ices, etc.—Juvenile literature   2. Ice cream industry—Juvenile literature   [1. Ice cream, ices, etc.   2. Ice cream industry]   I. Wolfe, Robert L.
II. Wolfe, Diane   III. Title   IV. Title: At the ice cream factory
      637'.4—dc22

ISBN 978-1-934545-06-5
Printed in the United States of America
12 11 10 09   4 3 2 1

Ice cream is delicious alone, with pie and cake, or sipped as a shake or malt. New flavors like raspberry chocolate truffle are being invented—and devoured—every day. Still, the most popular flavor of all time is vanilla. Come along! Find out how one factory makes this cold, creamy treat.

A tanker backs into the factory and unloads 5,500 gallons (20,820 liters) of fresh cream from the dairy.

The cream travels through pipes to storage **silos** inside the factory. The silos keep the cream refrigerated at 45 degrees Fahrenheit (7° C) or less.

Ingredients

Ice cream has two main ingredients: liquid sugar and cream. The mixture of sugar and cream, shown above, is called **raw mix.**

Pasteurization

Pasteurization is a process of heating ingredients to keep bacteria, or germs, from harming the raw mix. This company pasteurizes the raw mix in two ways. One method uses a High-Temperature Short-Time Pasteurizer (HTST). The HTST quickly heats the raw mix to 185 degrees Fahrenheit (85° C). Holding tubes keep the raw mix at that temperature for an additional 32.5 seconds. The extra heating time makes sure bacteria are held in check.

Batch Pasteurization Process

Big batches of the raw mix are pasteurized in vats, or large containers pictured above, that hold 1,000 gallons (3,785 liters) and 2,000 gallons (7,570 liters) of the raw mix. The raw mix is heated to a temperature of 155 degrees Fahrenheit (68° C) and maintained for 30 minutes.

Flavors

Employees add color and different flavors, such as vanilla, cotton candy, or egg custard, to vats. Here a worker adds vanilla to the mix.

Large turning blades called **agitators** stir the
flavors and colors into the mix.

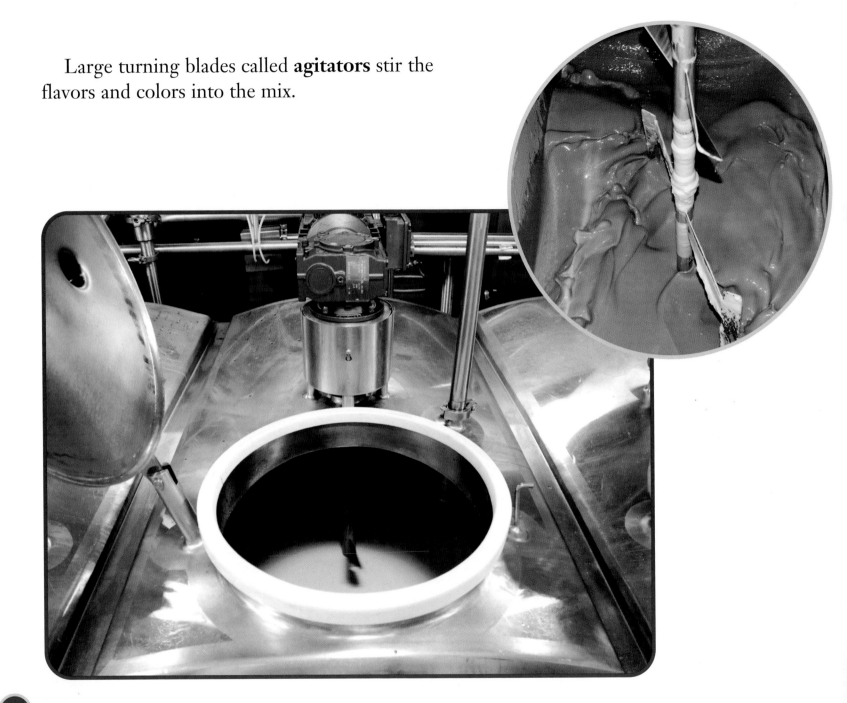

Freezing

Now the flavored mix is ready to go to the world's largest freezers. Each freezer can freeze up to 12,000 gallons (45,425 liters) of ice cream an hour! Large blades inside the freezers churn the ice cream as it gets thick and cold.

Special Swirls

Ribbons of flavor inside ice cream are called **variegates.** Some common variegates are fudge, fruit, caramel, or peanut butter. Variegates arrive at the factory in large barrels; some weigh more than 500 pounds (227 kilograms)!

Fruit, Candy & Nuts

Inclusions, which are bite-sized pieces of fruit, candy, and nuts, are added to the ice cream by a machine.

Nuts are stirred to keep them from clumping together. The amount and kind of inclusions added to the ice cream depends on the recipe being made at the time.

Chopped nuts spin quickly through the high-speed sifting machine before being added to the ice cream.

Filling

Ice cream comes in cartons of many shapes and sizes. Just the right amount of ice cream is squeezed from pipes into the cartons.

There are pints (0.47 liters), 1.5-quart **scrounds** (1.42 liters), and pails of both half-gallon (1.89 liters) and gallon (3.79 liters) sizes. Scrounds are oval-shaped packages.

Schools and restaurants often use containers filled with three gallons (11.36 liters) of ice cream. Three-gallon containers are sent to the freezer on metal guides that look like a roller coaster.

Freezing

Ice cream cartons move along a spiral conveyor to a special freezer called a hardener, where it's a chilly -20 degrees Fahrenheit (-29° C).

Cartons of ice cream stay in the hardener for two hours and fifteen minutes, until the ice cream is completely frozen.

Packaging

From the hardener, the ice cream travels along a conveyor to a machine that wraps plastic film from large rolls around each carton. This forms a safety seal around the carton.

The frozen containers of ice cream slide down a ramp and clunk together at the bottom in groups. A machine bundles the containers together for shipping.

Quality Inspection

The company wants to give each customer the best quality ice cream. Some cartons are taken off of the packaging ramp and inspected. The inspector checks that the ice cream has the right amount of inclusions.

Inspectors also check the ice cream to make sure it has the right balance of ingredients, including flavorings and sugar.

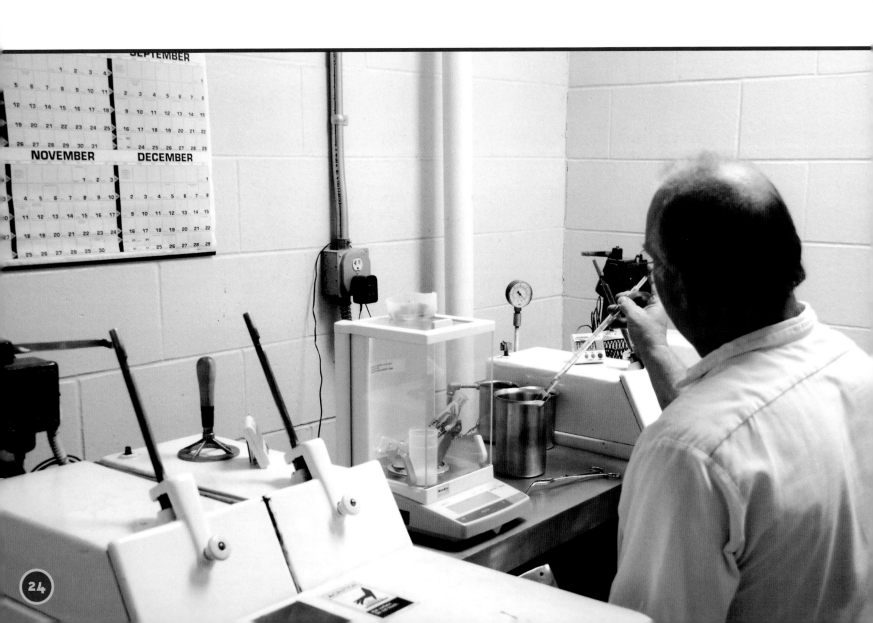

Ice Cream Sandwiches

A popular pre-made frozen treat is the ice cream sandwich. Here a worker loads a machine with chocolate wafer cookies.

A pump forces a pre-measured slab of ice cream downward, then cookies are automatically placed on each side to form an ice cream sandwich.

Boxes of ice cream sandwiches are grouped and bundled, then sent through a heated tunnel. The temperature in the tunnel is warm enough to shrink-wrap plastic quickly around the boxes, but not melt the ice cream.

Freezing Warehouse

Pallets of ice cream products are taken immediately to a large in-house freezer.

In the freezer, workers wear snowsuits and drive forklifts to transport the ice cream where it will be stored on shelves until it is shipped to a grocery store or restaurant.

Shipping

When the factory receives orders for ice cream, workers load the pallets or boxes inside a truck. A freezer unit blows cold air inside the truck so the ice cream stays frozen on its way to the grocery store.

At the grocery store, the cartons of ice cream are un-packed and displayed in a freezer case so customers can buy them for a sweet, creamy, satisfying treat any time of year.

Glossary

agitators: turning blades that stir flavors and colors into the mix

inclusions: bite-sized pieces of fruit, candy, and nuts

pasteurization: heating food ingredients for a specific time to kill harmful germs

raw mix: liquid sugar and cream that are the main ingredients for making ice cream

scrounds: rectangular-shaped containers with rounded corners

silos: large containers that hold ice cream

variegates: swirls of flavors such as fudge, fruit, caramel, or peanut butter

Index

Websites

www.kemps.com - Kemps LLC

www.idfa.org/facts/icecream/history.cfm - International Dairy Foods Association